THE TECHNIQUE OF FRESCO PAINTING

1. POMPEII. *The Passion. (detail)*
Photograph by Alinari.

THE TECHNIQUE OF FRESCO PAINTING

By GARDNER HALE

With additional Chapters prepared from Mr. Hale's notes by
SHAEMAS O'SHEEL
and a Preface by
JOSÉ CLEMENTE OROZCO

Dover Publications, Inc., New York

This Dover edition, first published in 1966, is an unabridged republication of the work originally published by William Edwin Rudge in 1933 under the former title: *Fresco Painting*.

Library of Congress Catalog Card Number: 66-15937

Manufactured in the United States of America

Dover Publications, Inc.
180 Varick Street
New York, N. Y. 10014

NOTE

The first ten chapters of this book were written by Mr. Hale, but, owing to his death, the last two chapters were written by Mr. Shaemas O'Sheel from Mr. Hale's voluminous notes. Mr. O'Sheel's work faithfully reflects the point of view of Mr. Hale, as will be readily appreciated by the reader.

PREFACE

THIS *book has something important to say and to give. It not only stands for a good cause but represents the experience of an artist who generously wants to share his valuable knowledge with others. Amid the confusion and the terrific noise, it is both timely and reassuring. Art is always produced in* silence, *as man himself is conceived and born, save for a few explosions of pleasure or pain.*

Now, after all the fuss, we may get down to actual facts—to the most simple facts. This work will help us to become more intimately acquainted with our pigments and the rest of our materials and help us also, by using them in perfect order, to keep order in our minds. That is precisely what our fellow painter, Gardner Hale, intended to show us.

Fresco has returned to demand a place in the intense social drama we are living today. In former times, the art of fresco was a religious ritual—an instrument used by the church for impressing the masses. Fresco painters were ordered to illustrate the Bible, to portray saints and martyrs, to describe the horrors of hell and the glories of a musical comedy heaven in pink, blue and gold. Nowadays, it is the hell of economic catastrophe and scientific destruction by modern warfare. Or, it is the imaginary heaven of a few idealists whose voices are all but lost in the universal maelstrom.

Again, fresco may assume its historic role in the contact between the artist and the masses. Again, it may be used freely for propagandizing new religions or industrial enterprises. High-powered commercial art may take the hint at any moment and launch fresco overnight for the strident advertising of tooth paste or radio equipment. The artist himself may prostitute the medium to broadcast his vanity and mediocrity. Fresco betrays everything behind the hand of the painter—weakness or power, knowledge or ignorance, taste or lack of it, vision or short-sightedness. But, at a time of uncertain standards, this quality of fresco to reveal, without subterfuge, the process of execution, the development of subject and the capacity of the painter, is invaluable in the swift discrimination between the false and the true. The artist, forced by strict discipline, must find out beforehand exactly what he wants to do and must prepare his designs and materials with thoroughness before the actual execution.

In these few lines, I wish to express my respect for an artist whom I, unfortunately, never met, but whom I understand and appreciate through the pursuit of a common craft. His book is destined, I believe, to help many artists by inducing them to learn a medium which is the oldest and still the best.

JOSÉ CLEMENTE OROZCO

BIOGRAPHICAL NOTE

Gardner Hale was born in Chicago, Illinois, February 1, 1894. His father was William Gardner Hale, and his mother was Harriet Knowles Swinburne Hale, who was a direct descendant of the poet Swinburne.

From the age of seven his exceptional art talent was conspicuous. During his early youth he was tutored by his father, in Rome, who was the first Director of the American School of Classical Studies, and a distinguished philologist. Gardner Hale studied with private teachers in America and in Europe. He graduated from the University High School of Chicago, then from Harvard University, in the class of 1914, and later from the Art Students League, in New York. Abroad he studied with Corlandi, A.S.L., at the Académie Julien in Paris, and with Maurice Denis.

After years of intensive research in the long neglected art of true fresco, he became a pioneer in the revival of fresco painting in America, where he employed his newly developed technique. Examples of Gardner Hale's work are in the Metropolitan Museum of Art, the Whitney Museum of American Art, in New York City, and in the Brooklyn Museum; also he did the mural decorations in the houses of Mr. Edward Shearson at Palm Beach, Mr. B. C. Work at Oyster Bay, Mr. Jay Carlisle at Islip, and Mrs. Christian R. Holmes at Sands Point, Long Island, and the Merchants Trust Building at Chicago. In Europe some of his commissions included the villas of Mr. L. M. Spelman and Mr. J. Walter Spalding, at Florence, Italy; the houses of Mrs. Walter Lewisohn and the Marquis Castel-Maurigi, at Paris; and the house of Mrs. William Payne Thompson, at London.

CONTENTS

I

II

TECHNIQUE

CONTENTS

PLATES

FRESCO PAINTING

2. MAYA. *Human Figures in the Temple of Warriors. (details) (a) Typical Warrior. (b) Head-dress of God Impersonator. (c) Member of the Maya Proletariat. (d) Seated Figure. From "The Temple of Warriors at Chichen-Itza, Yucatan." Volume II. Courtesy of the Carnegie Institute of Washington.*

Chapter I

DEFINITION

THE word fresco is constantly misused. Because of the clumsiness of the terms "mural painting" or "mural decoration" we have naturally come to speak of any wall painting as a fresco. But there is a more significant reason for this confusion: true fresco painting has been the principal and at times almost the only medium used for large scale wall decoration during the great art periods of the past.

Technically fresco is the name of a medium, like oils or water color. It consists of painting on freshly laid plaster with colors ground in water only. A medium is a binding material which makes the color adhere to the ground of canvas, paper, stone, wood, plaster or whatever the surface to be painted. In oils the colors are ground in linseed oil and the drying of this substance attaches the color. In water-color, gum arabic is the medium. The basis of tempera painting is egg, either the yolk or the white or both together, alone or in combination with other materials. Then there are size painting, glue painting, wax painting, milk painting and countless others. The juice of the fig tree has been used with success, and rubber, which is related to it, may have a great future.

But in fresco the medium, if it can be so called, is the fresh plaster itself. I use the word plaster to mean a coating of lime and sand or cement and sand as the term is commonly employed in America and England but never to mean gypsum plaster or plaster of Paris.

Each day a piece of the finish coat is laid of the size which the artist can finish before night. The next day the color would no longer hold. On this plaster he paints with colors which have been ground with water only. The paint penetrates the surface, is incorporated with it, and the two dry together. It does not sink in deeply as is sometimes supposed, but the natural crystalline surface of the plaster forms like a glass on the color and fixes it absolutely.

Thus the "true fresco" painting (the Italians call it *buon fresco*) is built up piece by piece, each one completed before the next is started. The divisions are made to follow contours in the design and each day's work is fitted to the others much as one sets together the sections of a picture puzzle.

There has been much exaggerated talk about the permanence of fresco and a good deal of nonsense written. Eternity is a very large word—charming because incomprehensible. Painting is far less lasting than sculpture. If this were not so we should still have many Greek pictures, of which there was an abundance. A thousand years is a long life for a painting.

Fresco is the most permanent medium for walls. Its beauty increases with age, and given proper protection it can easily see its thousand years. A painting in some other medium on a separate panel of wood or copper plate or even on canvas may live longer, for it has an isolated life surrounded by air. But fresco fights its battle on the wall and a wall is subject to all kinds of disasters, from faulty construction and crumbling and destruction of the material to dampness and the germ which it breeds—saltpetre. Saltpetre is a veritable disease of the wall. It destroys all painting which is exposed to it. It is the principal cause of the loss of the great masterpieces of the past. The well-known case of Leonardo's Last Supper is only one in a thousand.

Fresco, because of its unique applicability to the wall, has had all the responsibility of this struggle with saltpetre and it has resisted far better than other media.

It has also been called permanent out of doors. It is washable and consequently unaffected by rain, and extraordinarily resistent to the direct rays of the sun. But on the outside of a house it cannot hope for more than a hundred years of good condition and two or three hundred more of faded charm. Dust, inner moisture in the wall, and the chemical constituents of the air, salt near the sea and the sulphur and other gases of the cities, are its deadly enemies.

During the sixteenth and seventeenth centuries, quantities of houses in North Italy were painted in fresco. Only a few traces remain. Giorgione painted the facade of his house in Venice—where is it now?

The outdoor use of fresco will always be limited. But its possibilities indoors are endless. Probably the oldest mural medium in the world, it still has the greatest future. From the time lime plaster was first used, men must have experimented in painting on it while it was wet—to save time if for no other reason—and been delighted to find that the color held without the addition of any binding material. As long as walls are finished in plaster it will always be the more appropriate and beautiful method of ornamenting them. This comes from the fact that it is not a coating on the wall but the surface of the wall itself, as intimately a part of its structure as the skin is of the body.

Fresco has been called a lost art. This is not true. Its use survives generally in a rather debased form in most of the countries of Europe. But although the principle is there, it has sunk sadly from its past glorious position as the leader among media.

Its technique, forced by the difficulty of the material, was carried over into other ways of painting and gave them their backbone. Even the dangerously easy and consequently in itself undistinguished medium of oils was influenced for centuries by the sturdy and virile technique of fresco. In fact, the decadence of oil corresponds with the dying out of this influence.

One could almost write a history of the painting of the Middle Ages and the Renaissance, judging it entirely from its relation to technical skill in fresco. It is true that tempera painting follows the same line. One was for monumental work on walls, the other for separate panels where lime plaster could not be used. But this egg-painting was always made for a definite place, usually an altar-piece, and its conception was invariably decorative. The method was practically identical for both. So fresco should be considered the big brother of the two. It had the responsibility and should have the glory of the great development from the thirteenth century onward.

The line of ascent and descent is very clear. With Giotto and his contemporaries and their immediate followers, fresco blossoms out into its full flower, never to be surpassed technically. The grounds are perfectly prepared, fine smooth plaster, very thin, very compressed by expert troweling. The colors, thoroughly ground, are the great traditional palette, simple, noble, permanent. The whole thing is essentially fresco. It could not have been conceived, certainly could not have been executed, in any other medium.

Then the line goes on through Masaccio with his mysterious and beautiful technique, through Fra Angelico, that great technician, Benozzo Gozzoli and Ghirlandaio, who would both have been mediocre painters had they not been great frescoists, until finally we reach Michael Angelo. Then the line descends rapidly.

There are hundreds of foolish legends about Michael Angelo's ignorance of fresco. We are told in a dozen ways that when he undertook the ceiling of the Sistine Chapel, because he was ignorant of the technique, he employed painters to come and execute his pieces before him and that he would then destroy them and begin again. In this story is the key to all the absurd libel. He tried to employ assistants, for the undertaking was enormous, and because their work was inadequate he had to send them away. His conception was too new, and let us admit that his nature was difficult. But it is ridiculous to suppose that a man brought up as he was in the workshops of Florence who had even been appointed to Ghirlandaio, that almost too perfect technician, was ignorant of the medium.

But the proof is in the work itself. The most casual examination, even a photograph, shows it to be the purest fresco.

Curiously enough, his gracious and gifted contemporary, Raphael, shows the first signs of decline in the handling of the medium. Of course he knew it well, but it is almost a case of familiarity breeding contempt. There was much work to do and life was joyous. The shop was working overtime and the result was soft, thick, porous plaster and poorly ground color. Immediately we see for the first time that chalky, dead look which results from these two great faults.

Fresco never recovered. In the next generation we find the genial Vasari talking enthusiastically of the medium, quoting Michael Angelo as saying that it was the only manner of painting fit for a man and yet doing work himself which, for distinction of color, might have been executed in kalsomine.

And so it goes. The deep resonant tone of the early fresco disappears until our own time. The medium was on the decline. Oil painting with its easy effects was driving it out. The easel painting had come in; that is, a painting conceived independently of its ultimate placement. And yet the great Venetian masters who were largely responsible for this change,

Giorgione, Titian, Veronese, Tintoretto and even El Greco who was trained in Venice, were all schooled in fresco as the principal traditional medium and were only taught oil painting as an innovation. In all their work they kept the essentially fresco qualities—a logically developed painting within a rigidly predetermined drawing, carried from beginning to end with a definite purpose, free from hesitations and corrections. Their method of underpainting in cool tones and working over this with the local color descends directly from Giotto.

In the eighteenth century there was a last flowering of fresco in Tiepolo. His chalky tone of color is, if anything, rather worse than that of the Vasari school. And yet what really monumental painting it is and what an essentially fresco conception! The genius of Tiepolo coming in that time of small inconsequences, of "nice shades and fine feeling", is one of the great accidents of history. With him fresco flares up and dies. We must take our spark to-day, not from the almost extinct tradition of the nineteenth century, but from the great period between Giotto and Michael Angelo.

And so we come to America, for the future of the fresco and, I believe, of painting in general lies there. I have lived a large part of my life abroad and have a great admiration for the modern painting of Europe. It has an honesty, a directness, and a comprehension of form which can be compared without exaggeration to the best work of the past. But it prides itself on its technical ignorance and despises any decorative utility. This unfortunate tendency comes from the fact that there is really practically no monumental work to be done and the artist has been forced into an attitude, not unlike the traditional one of "sour grapes", of believing that the smaller and more useless, decoratively speaking, his pictures, the more significant they must be. Before the work of the best man in

Paris to-day, I have a feeling that I am seeing fragments, often magnificently painted, but details, sketches for some large conception which is never to be carried out.

We in America have the work to be done. Never since the Renaissance has there been a country which so definitely needed mural painting. Everything is new. Architecture is developing extraordinarily. Everywhere there is no longer the luxury of an eccentric as in Europe but an actual social and economic necessity. A really first rate bank can no longer afford to cover its walls with the cheap plaster work and "house painting" of another generation. The same is true of the office building, the railway station, and countless other forms of modern construction. This work has to be done, and it should be a joy to the American artist to realize that his painting corresponds to an economic need. I do not mean that life is a bed of roses for him. His existence is extraordinarily precarious. And yet, in spite of this, we are building up a group of painters who will be able to meet the problem. I don't mean the portrait painters, the landscape painters, the marine painters, or even the snowscene painters — thank Heaven the cow painter has died out — but just plain painters in the fine old sense of the word.

One reason things are not developing more rapidly is that the business man who usually has the giving out of work in his hands is suspicious of the sickly, sentimental type which he supposes the artist to be. He has a contract to give for work to be completed in such and such a place for such and such a price and, above all, by such and such a time. He expects these conditions to be fulfilled as exactly as by a plumber. I have nothing against the noble art of the plumber and I have no doubt that he also fulfills his contract. In fact, I prefer the plumber type of painter to that sad hangover of the nineteenth century—the misunderstood artist. In this I am only preferring the type which comes closest to the great artists of the Renaissance.

Not that I think the American business man is perfect. He is "cock-sure," uneducated in matters of art, unwilling to trust a specialist in another line, although he may be ready to employ him at a large price because he is a specialist. But underneath, he is profoundly wistful and yearning. This is a quality for which Europe does not give him credit. It sees only the "hard-boiled" protective front or, as a contrast to it, the soft sentimentality which is the rather nauseating result of this wistfulness when combined with an untrained mind. But on the whole he is as he should be: hard, reserved, suspicious, waiting "to be shown." And he is "being shown" by the fact that he cannot put up a good modern building without employing artists. It enhances his respect for them exceedingly.

Of the so-called public buildings, the less said the better. An earlier generation for which I have the greatest admiration except as artists has already covered them with its noble and very bad paintings.

In the private house the development is more rapid. There is no great responsibility there, not even a large expenditure. The result has been a series of experiments which are in most part highly successful. There are more decorated dining rooms, hallways and bath rooms, not to mention loggias and even swimming pools, dotted about the country than one would have any idea of, and most of this work is good.

In the last ten years America has leaped into a position of world prominence. Our power, our wealth (to put it crudely) has to be expressed. Every country since the beginning of history when it found itself in a position similar to ours has felt an overpowering urge for self-expression. History as we know it, in fact, is principally a record of just these efforts towards a race culture. The work of art survives long after

3. BYZANTINE. *Saint Ephraem and a Monk. (detail)*
From "Dormition of Saint Ephraem" in Dochiarou, Athos.
From "Monuments de L'Athos" by Gabriel Millet. Courtesy of the publisher, Ernest Leroux, Paris.

4. GIOTTO (1266-1336). *Saint Francis.*
From the fresco at Assisi. Photograph by Anderson of Rome.

5. MASACCIO (1401-1428). *The Tribute Money. (detail)*
From the fresco in the church del Carmine at Florence. Photograph by Anderson of Rome.

6. PIERO DELLA FRANCESCA (1416-1492). *The Women of the Queen of Sheba. (detail)*
From the fresco in the church of Saint Francis at Arezzo. Photograph by Anderson of Rome.

7. D. GHIRLANDAIO (1449-1498). *The Birth of the Virgin. (detail)*
From the fresco in the church of Santa Maria Novella at Florence. Photograph by Maneilli & Co.

8. GIOVANNI BATTISTA TIEPOLO (1696-1770). *Apotheosis. (detail: upper half)*
From the fresco in the Palazzo Rezzonico at Venice.

the battle is forgotten. Or if the battle is remembered, it is because sculpture or painting has immortalized it. Our national culture is coming and coming rapidly, as all things move to-day. Our conditions require mural painting, and within relatively few years we should have a school of frescoists, able to express our aims, our ideas, and our national aspirations.

But if you were to go into any art shop to-day and ask for materials for fresco, the chances are that the dealer would not know what you were talking about or he might sell you some horrible concoction with "fresco" as a trade name. Yet the materials are simple and as common as they ever were. In fact, for certain things America is probably better equipped than was Italy in the fourteenth century. It is to assist you in finding and judging these materials that this book has been written.

The author has painted in fresco for the past sixteen years in Italy, France and America. He has had an unusual opportunity for the comparative study of materials in these different countries and has searched America to find those which are most perfectly suited. He hopes that his fellow artist, after reading this book, will experiment in fresco. Some at least will find the means of expression of which they have dreamed. Other younger men and women by working in fresco from the beginning of their studies may be saved years of searching and experimentation. Others who are not artists but who are interested in mural decoration, either for its glorious past or for its significant future, may be interested in gaining an intimate knowledge of this most fascinating and noble medium.

Chapter II

THE WALL

THE foundation on which the plaster for our painting is to go is of the greatest importance, for the life of a fresco is that of its ground. This may be of brick, stone, concrete, hollow tile, wire lath, or any material on which a lime or cement plaster can be securely laid. Wood lath is not safe because of the expansion and contraction and its tendency to strike through the finish coat. The wood holds moisture and this collects dust on the surface, so that after a few years the plaster has a striped effect.

The Renaissance frescoes were mostly done on brick or stone. The walls of the Villa Razzolini in Florence which I painted were of a typical fourteenth century construction: great arches of brick filled in with various kinds of stone, brick, and rubble. Many fine paintings have been done on such grounds but, generally speaking, uniformity of material is a great advantage. Stone is less absorbent than brick or tile, cement less so than lime. Such a mixed ground causes an uneven suction in the finish coat of plaster, making the trowelling more difficult, and retarding the setting in spots.

Even with brick or hollow tile, it is advisable that they should be as evenly baked as possible. An underbaked brick is very absorbent; an overbaked one will keep the plaster above it wet for hours.

Concrete has little suction and in this resembles a hard stone.

Wire lath, now so commonly used in America, is excellent foundation. It has the fault of making the plaster dry rather quickly; but its suction is uniform, and it has the great advantage of being practically proof against saltpetre. It is also ideal for making portable panels.

But the artist usually has little choice in the matter of grounds for, as a rule, the wall already exists before he is called in. What he must determine is whether the wall is sound. It is relatively easy to see if the structure is solid. What is more difficult is to detect the presence of saltpetre. Look the wall over very carefully. If you see any dark, moist-looking stains or any salty efflorescence, scratch the spot to the depth of a quarter of an inch or more and take this dust to a chemist to be analysed for potassium nitrate (KNO_3).

If there is saltpetre, refuse to work on the wall as it stands. Your painting is doomed on such a ground no matter what the medium. The only safe remedy is to construct a facing of wire lath or even tile, leaving an air space of an inch or more between it and the wall. If space does not permit of this projection, the old wall can usually be cut away sufficiently to allow for it. The different modern waterproofing and tar products to stop inner dampness in the masonry are not safe. The ancients used a sheet of lead but without much success.

The wall must be "trued up" and have its joints filled. Any irregularities will take away from the bond of the plaster. It should nevertheless not be smooth. In the case of finished stone it is advisable to roughen up the surface with a cold chisel.

Although fresco is essentially a mural medium there are cases when it is necessary to make transportable panels. They are also ideal for practice or study. The best ground for this is wire lath or even fine chicken wire, stretched on a frame. Over this a rough or "scratched" coat of plaster is laid, and when this is dry, the finish coat can be put on as on a wall. In the case of a small panel—i.e., one that can be finished in a day's painting—a deep single coat is enough and has the advantage of far greater solidity.

For permanent work the stretcher or frame should be of

L-shaped iron, called angle iron, the depth allowing for the thickness of two coats of plaster. For ordinary work and experiments a wooden frame is satisfactory with the wire lath simply tacked to the back.

Fresco can also be done on a large tile such as is used for roofs, or on a slate, although with the latter the adhesion is less good.

Chapter III

THE PLASTER

THIS wall must now receive one or more coats of plaster before it is ready for the fresco painter. Good American specifications call for two preparatory coats, the "scratched" and the "brown" coat. One properly made is enough except on wire lath. The old frescoists rarely used more. These coats should be made of lime and sand, or lime, cement and sand, in the general proportion of one part of lime, or lime and cement, to two parts of sand. The surface should be left rough, that is to say, sand-finished. I personally like my "brown" coat slightly scratched as it gives a better bond for the finish plaster.

This is the condition in which a wall is usually turned over to the fresco painter by the contractor or builder.

From now on the artist must watch his materials closely and know them intimately, for the success of his work largely depends on their purity and the skill of their application.

The finish coat on which he is to paint, laying a piece day by day, is made of lime (or cement) and sand, like the preceding ones. But their quality must be of the finest and they must be scrupulously clean.

There are two general types of lime, the "fat" or "quick" lime and the hydraulic. The former is the traditional unique material for fresco and is undoubtedly the best to-day. The hydraulic limes have the advantage of somewhat greater strength; but they dry too rapidly to permit of a day's work, and they are usually somewhat tinted, either grey or rose. For certain limited effects this ground color may be useful.

The cements are the grey Portland and the relatively new white cement. The latter is the one which is useful for fresco because of its color. But as, like all cements, it dries very rapidly, it should only be added in small quantities to the lime in order to give greater strength.

Lime is the universal fresco material. It can be bought in lumps and slaked in the old-fashioned manner by adding water. This is a difficult process, and few workmen are skilled at it nowadays. There is with it always the danger of pitting. Little unslaked particles after a few months in contact with the humidity of the air break off bits of the surface, leaving white spots.

I advise you to use the modern hydrated lime,* of which there are several excellent brands in America. It comes in a powdered form, sealed in paper sacks of fifty pounds. Both lime and cement should be very fresh. Any lumpiness is a sign that they are stale. This lime can be mixed dry with the sand and water added to make up the plaster or "stuff" as the plasterers call it; or it can be mixed with water into a paste or "putty" to be kept in a barrel or pit. Aging it in this way improves its plasticity. In Florence I found lime which had been kept for five years, and it was extraordinarily pleasant to handle. But this is a luxury we are not likely to meet with in America. It is a good thing, however, to keep the mixed "stuff" of lime and sand at least over night. It should, of course, be reworked in the morning before it is used.

The other important element in the plaster is the sand. It should be put through a fine screen. Avoid all sand which has been taken from a beach or too near the sea, as well as that which is too earthy. It should in any case be washed. This is done by stirring it in a barrel in which there is a running hose. A small quantity may be stirred up in a pail and the water

* The lime of the wet plaster combines with the carbonic acid of the air through the thin coating of the applied pigment, and this chemical process is facilitated by the water of the wet plaster. The period of evaporation varies according to the conditions.

poured off. After this has been done a few times, the water should be quite clear. It must then be dried before being used.

The sand should be angular, rather than round, and of the ordinary brown color, as this gives the most pleasing tone to the plaster. White sand produces an unpleasant cold tint and as it is usually beach sand it is also dangerous because of the salt it contains. Marble dust, although much talked about in connection with fresco, has been relatively little used. It is not necessary as a fine marble-like surface can be made with the ordinary sand. It also has the disadvantage of "pitting".

The mixture of lime and sand for the plaster is one part of the former to two of the latter. This traditional proportion, however, really applies to lime in the "putty" or paste state. For the dry hydrated lime it is better to make it a little "fatter" by increasing the dose. For a dry mixture the proportion of five parts lime to eight of sand is a good one. The mixture had best be determined "at the job" as the freshness of the lime and the fineness of the sand must be considered. The proportions once decided upon, however, they should be maintained exactly throughout the entire work.

A "fat" plaster is easier to trowel and to bring up to a smooth surface; but it has a tendency to crack. Also the colors do not take as easily as on a "lean" one.

If you are mechanically inclined (and an artist is likely to be), if you like the feel of a tool and are stimulated by the skillful use of it, you will find these apparently dull details interesting. I was enthralled by the mechanics of this medium from the time I first started experimenting in it, and I still find them extraordinarily fascinating. Other artists who do not know the joy of "doing things with their hands" need only understand the principles of what constitutes a sound ground and sound materials. But even they should experiment a little in plastering.

The actual laying and trowelling of the day's piece of the finish coat in fresco is of vital importance to the success of the painting. A little question of the wetting of the wall, the working up of the plaster, the laying, the "scouring," the trowelling will make all the difference in the result of your day's work.

In large scale work all this must be done by a mechanic, and any good plasterer is able to do it with a little training. But you must be capable of showing him how. He will start by despising you as an artist, which to him means a hopelessly impractical person, and he will never pay the slightest attention to your direction unless you can take the trowel yourself.

The wetting of the wall is always a problem. Brick and tile should be soaked down. Very absorbent walls in summer should be wet the evening before and again in the morning. Stone and concrete or cement need only be moistened with a brush. Walls of mixed materials will need more water here and less there. You will come to know the wet and the dry spots in your ground. A part insufficiently moistened cannot be trowelled to a smooth finish. A wet spot cannot be painted on for hours, and as you must finish before night this is often disastrous.

The "stuff" or plaster must be worked up or beaten with the least possible amount of water and the greatest possible amount of energy. Here you will always have trouble with your plasterer because it is a question of hard physical work. Too much water in this mixture makes it easier to handle, but the resulting surface is weak and takes the color badly. And, far more important, it sets so slowly that you lose hours of your precious day. Your plasterer will refuse to believe, until you have proved it to him, that mixing the "stuff" for a long time, really beating it, with the least possible amount of water, makes it more malleable and plastic in the end than his ordinary method of drowning it. It should be of the consistency of butter not cream.

This material, then, is placed on the square board called a "hawk" which the plasterer holds in his left hand, and with the trowel of his right he applies it to the wall. There is a trick to this which you will learn. After letting it stand for a few minutes according to the suction of the ground, he takes a small rectangular piece of wood a little larger than a playing card and about a quarter of an inch thick, with a handle attached to the back (it is called a "scourer") and rubs all over the surface, evening it up and adding plaster wherever it is necessary. If the ground has been properly moistened he should not have to add water during this process.

Then as quickly as possible he trowels up the surface to a smooth finish. The best tool for this is a small, slightly flexible, pointed trowel, about five inches long. Remember you are only plastering a piece you can paint in a day and your tools must be fine, particularly when it comes to approaching the finish piece of the day before.

So now you have your wall ready to paint on but before starting, I must tell you about your colors and how they are ground.

Chapter IV

THE COLORS

THE fresco palette is very limited as the only colors which can be used are those which resist the alkaline action of the lime. They are the oxides of iron and a few other minerals. This at first will seem a great disadvantage to those who are accustomed to working in other media. Particularly the painter in oils will regret the bright tints which this dark unluminous material has forced him to use. But you must remember that because fresco is essentially mural and architectural, a certain restraint is inherent to its beauty.

The colors today are fundamentally those which Giotto and Leonardo used. All the oxides of iron are the same. The *azzurro della magna* is replaced by cobalt. Their chemical properties are somewhat similar, their difficulty of handling and tonal effect are very much the same. The old ultramarine—genuine lapis lazuli—which gave such extraordinarily noble and resonant tones—has had to be replaced, except for very special work, by the artificial ultramarine or Guimet blue, which is said to be exactly the same chemically but which alas! perhaps because it lacks the impurities of the original has not its dignity and reserve.

Amatito or *amatisto* was in all probability a burnt oxide of iron. Mars violet resembles it very closely and gives the same fine madder-like purple and mauves.

Much has been written about the famous "lost red"—sinopia. I have been enormously interested in the question of this so-called lost color which is said to have been responsible for the magnificent reds in the old paintings and I have had chemists assist me in a search for it. I believe the sinopia legend has arisen in part from a confusion about the old reds, natural quicksilver vermilions (cinnabar) and the finest forms of the red oxides of iron, having been classed together. But the principal confusion has come from the fact that those who have written of this color have not practised fresco. The clarity and intensity of colors in this medium are incredible to anyone who has not actually painted in it. The principal red oxide of iron is what is known to-day as light red. Everyone who has worked in oils knows that although this color when mixed with a great deal of white may give a useful flesh tone, used with any intensity it only makes a dirty red. In fresco it will give almost all the range from a vermilion to a madder, In the same way a fine yellow ochre is more beautiful on the wall than a medium cadmium or an orange cadmium when mixed with light red.

In this lies one of the great secrets of the beauty of fresco. The more restrained colors, carefully chosen for their greatest purity, are used at their highest intensity and this accounts for their incomparable solidity and dignity of tone. In oils the process is likely to be quite the opposite. Intense colors have to be down, producing that hollow and unpleasant tonality which the French call "éclairé en dedans."

Two thoroughly solid modern colors are very useful—viridian and light or lemon cadmium.

Here is a list of safe and essentially fresco colors:

Lime White	*Van Dyck Red*
Antimony Yellow	*Raw Umber*
Cadmium Yellow, light	*Burnt Umber*
Yellow Ochre	*Terra Verde*
Raw Sienna	*Malachite Green*
Burnt Sienna	*Viridian*
Pezzuole Red	*Cobalt Green*
Light Red	*Cobalt Blue*
Venetian Red	*Ultramarine*

My own palette is: lime white, light cadmium, yellow ochre, pezzuole red, light red, Mars violet, raw umber, terra verde, viridian, cobalt blue, ultramarine.

I have purposely left out the blacks although they are all permanent because they are unsatisfactory and tend to give a mottled effect. Also they are entirely out of the tone of the fresco coloration. I used a mixed black of ultramarine, raw umber and Mars violet. This combination is so intense that it usually has to be lighted with a good deal of white.

The only white in fresco is lime. This color is in great part responsible for its unique beauty and permanence. This material of the wall itself, mixed with the colors, binds the two together and makes the painting an intimate part of the wall. It is a fine quality of the same lime used in the plastering, carefully ground. The Florentine painters of the Renaissance went through a complicated process of grinding it, drying it over a long period and grinding it again. It was then known as *bianco sangiovanni.*

This completes the list of colors which you will probably use when you are familiar with the medium. But until you have learned to have confidence in their adequacy, you will want to experiment with a number of others which are said to be sound by chemists. They are dark cadmium, zinc yellow, strontian yellow and rose madder. All the Mars colors are permanent but aside from the violet they offer very little that you cannot get from ochre, light red, the siennas and umber.

The colors are bought in form of powder by weight. The greatest care must be taken to get only the purest. This is difficult in America, as powdered colors when sold at retail are used almost entirely for house painting and are consequently likely to be adulterated. Permanence is of no importance in such work and the temptation to touch up an inferior quality of pigment with a bit of bright ephemeral color must be enormous.

THE COLORS

These colors may be used in powder as they are bought with the simple admixture of water. Those who paint in frescoes to-day usually adopt this system, and it was the common practice of the painter of the seventeenth and eighteenth centuries. I believe it to be the greatest mistake. The later frescoes all have a chalky appearance which destroys most of the dignity of the medium, and this is largely caused by unground color. As reliable, ready-prepared fresco colors do not as yet exist, the only thing to do is to grind them or have them ground yourself.

For small quantities this is not uninteresting work and it gives a remarkable familiarity with the characteristics—what one might call the "habits" of each pigment. Some are thin and transparent, others fat and opaque. Some require little water, others a surprising amount.

For a large commission you will find it best to have someone in your studio to do this work. But you will have to have had some experience in order to instruct him.

Your tools are a plaque of ground glass about eighteen inches square, a muller of glass about the size and shape of a pear with the large end cut off flat, and a rather stiff, straight palette knife. You put a small quantity of the color on the plaque and add enough water to make it the consistency of thick cream. Then with the muller you work it round and round, drawing it towards the centre from time to time with the knife. You will see a marked change in the texture and even the color. Remember, the longer you grind the finer will be the tonality of your painting. Now gather the pigment up with your knife and put it in a jelly glass or wide-mouthed jar with a top. Always keep the surface covered with water.

There is a trick to the motion of grinding. Don't get discouraged if you are awkward at first—you will be surprised to find how rapidly you become proficient.

Chapter V

THE CARTOON

IT is almost impossible to carry out a fresco without having prepared a full scale drawing. There can be no hesitation, no mistakes, for the only correction possible is to destroy the day's piece and begin again the next morning. When you add to this the fact that you are working always against time in order to finish before dark, you will readily see that the idea must be studied out in advance to the last detail. Also as a fresco is built up piece by piece, some kind of guide is necessary in order to fit them together.

Until the fifteenth century, this composition was made directly on the brown coat, sketched out first in charcoal and then outlined with red ochre. This was difficult on a ground sufficiently rough to give a good bond for the finish coat, and it is interesting to see how they tended to make the brown coat too smooth. The other defect of this system was that the preliminary drawing was always concealed by the finish coat of the day. This was not altogether a misfortune, as the artist was forced to work from memory—to improvise, as it were, under strictly limited conditions, between the finished piece of the day before and the definitely determined piece of the morrow.

The other advantage of this system was that the composition was created on the wall itself with the scale and color of the building under the artist's eye.

The painters of the full Renaissance designed their work on sheets of paper pasted together. Modern paper, coming as it does in long rolls and widths of four feet and more, is ideally convenient.

Your own taste and the character of your work will define

for you how developed your cartoon should be. It may be merely an indication of the large design or it may be a highly detailed and finished study of every object. Remember that every bit of work you do on the cartoon is saved for the finished painting, not in the same sense that you are to make a slavish copy. On the contrary, because all this preliminary work has given you a complete mental image of what you propose to do, you are free to improvise and embroider to your heart's content. It is the perfect case of the much talked of freedom through discipline. You will be surprised to see how little you will bother to look at the cartoon of the bit on which you are actually working; that is, if you are a good painter. If you are not, not even fresco can make you one.

Your cartoon must now be pieced to make a pounce. Lay under it a piece of paper of the same size and pin the two together. The thinner these two papers are, especially the second, the better. Under them you place a folded piece of stuff or a small, smooth rug, and on a large table or on the floor according to the size of the work and your own temperament, you prick the cartoon. The traditional and best implement for this is a medium sized needle introduced into a split end of a short piece of old paint brush handle and bound up with thread. The pricking will seem extraordinarily tedious labor to you at first, but you will be astonished to see how fast you can go after a little practice. You will find that the closer the pricking, the more rapid the movement because it is continuous. For straight lines or large curves, a fine dressmaker's wheel is most useful.

The second sheet, which in this way becomes the duplicate of your cartoon, is now laid over the brown coat and a small muslin bag filled with charcoal dust is rubbed over it. This process of pouncing leaves the design in fine black points on the brown coat. The lines are then traced with light red and water. This red ochre is the best for tracing, for by its nature it fixes itself so well that even the wetting down of the wall does not disturb it. It may also be used for the *pounce* but this is not advisable, as the dust penetrates everything and with the least moisture it will spoil your floor.

You must save your duplicate cartoon in order to cut it up, following the daily pieces, and pounce this bit of your design on the finish coat.

There is another way of transferring your cartoon to the wall. You simply place your drawing over the fresh piece and trace the contour with a pointed steel instrument. This leaves an inducted line in the plaster. This is of little use in large work as it will not help you to get your design on to the brown coat, but it is good for small panels or to transfer variations or additions which do not exist in your cartoon. Its fault is that the line will persist, no matter what changes you make during the painting. Although it is hardly visible at first, with the dust of time it becomes very marked.

But the time given to grinding and pricking is not so much lost creatively as may first appear, for while you are thus occupied yet not preoccupied, you can give your mind up entirely to the working out of the last detail of your scheme. For on the morrow when you start your fresco, if you have not already completely painted it in your head, you will fail. Try grinding facing your cartoon. The movement of the hand clears and frees the brain. It is an ideal moment to plan.

Later, when you have that great commission, you will have a boy in your studio to do the grinding and pricking and may regret the quiet limpid days when you did it all yourself. But that is also a question of temperament.

Chapter VI

BRUSHES

THERE is some difficulty in finding satisfactory brushes for fresco. The old masters used larger ones of pigs' bristles and fine ones made from squirrels' tails. Cennino describes the making of brushes from old bristles which have previously been used in a much larger brush with which the wall was dampened. This manner of breaking in the bristles must have softened them.

The ordinary brush of the "Rubens" type is useful. Devoe and Company have a brush, known as a "Fresco Striper," made of pigs' bristles which comes in many sizes and is very useful. It has the end cut on a diagonal and was probably intended for decorators for "striping" or working with a straight edge. Devoe and other firms also have a long soft brush known as a "Rigger" which is excellent for fine work. Also, the Japanese brushes, particularly the larger ones, are very good.

In France and Italy they have a good brush made of calves' hair, and in the latter country there can also be found long, round, springy bristle brushes intended for "striping."

The essentials in a brush for fresco are: first, that it should not curl up through the alkaline action of the lime; and second, that it should be able to contain a great deal of liquid. Also it must have the elasticity to spring back even when nearly empty.

Chapter VII

PAINTING

NOW you are ready to paint. The plaster has been laid the very first thing in the morning following a line which you have traced a few inches beyond the edge of the piece which you plan to paint so as to allow for a clean cut. You have begun at the upper left hand corner of your wall; left, because if you use a mahlstick it will rest on the unpainted brown coat; at the top, so that the water will not run over the finish work when you wet the brown coat for your next piece and stain it.

Your ground colors in the glasses are arranged, as on a palette, at the back of a large table. It is a good idea to tack a little thin edging about the sides of the table to keep them from falling off. You have also about two dozen small jelly glasses in which to mix your colors. This is none too many as all your tones must be made in them. On the table there is also a small pitcher with clean water to add to the colors, and within reach is a pailful of water to rinse the brushes.

You now cut from the double of the cartoon the piece which corresponds to your day's work and pounce it on to the fresh plaster. For this you can use the same charcoal black as before or light red. But the best is terra verde in powder, for it is dark when wet from the moisture of the wall but dries very much lighter and therefore is hardly visible in the finished work.

The plaster must be firm before you do this pouncing. Otherwise the paper laid over will call the moisture to the surface, spoiling your pounce by filling up the holes, and also weakening the plaster. It is in having the plaster trowel easily and yet set rapidly and firmly that all your skill in its preparation and laying will come into play.

In deciding on the contours of your day's piece, remember that a curved line is less visible than a straight one; that it will show less in a dark passage than in a light; and that the cut must not be too complicated. The placing of these joints will come to be a relatively simple matter after a little experience. They are hard to find in the work of Renaissance painters although they made no great effort to conceal them. In my own work, even with the memory of how it was done, I am sometimes at a loss to follow them out.

If your cartoon is cut to the exact size of your piece you can mark its outline by passing a brush filled with color, preferably terra verde, over the edges. Now with a steel knife, or what is called a "small tool," cut to this line, scraping off whatever plaster projects beyond it. With a fine brush and very liquid terra verde trace over the dotted lines from your pounce.

Now I must leave you to your own devices with a blessing and a prayer that you may finish the piece before dark. There are as many ways of painting in fresco as in any other medium and you will have to work out your own style for yourself.

But there are a few rules. Do not clog your ground. The beauty of the medium depends on the white of the plaster illuminating the semi-transparent pigment, as does the light in a fine old stained glass which time has made half opaque. Your work should have the brilliance of a water color and yet the distinction of solid painting, for your pigments are mixed with white. So keep your colors liquid so that your brush, lifted from the glass, sheds drops freely. Get your intensity of tone by passing it several times, allowing five minutes or more to let it set. The warm tones you can pass two or three times. The cool many more. Preserve the transparency and yet keep your ground covered evenly. A thin passage will look cold and harsh as the plaster whitens in drying. At the same time allow for the fact that all your colors will grow more opaque as they set.

You will need to mix about five variations for each color — three principal tones, one lighter still, and the other darker than the darkest. All the colors dry lighter but not all to the same degree. This change is peculiar to fresco and not the same as in tempera or in size painting. On general principles, the dark oxides of iron—light red, burnt sienna and particularly the umbers — change relatively little. Colors mixed with a great deal of white and above all, terra verde, change surprisingly.

The mixtures cannot be kept for the next day as the lime in them thickens and they do not work so well and, more important, the bond is less good. So every evening what is left is thrown away and the glasses washed, and in the morning you have the problem of mixing fresh colors to match the work of the day before which has started to dry and looks decidedly strange, or the work of two or more days before which is already approximating its final tone several shades lighter than what you must mix.

This seems like an almost insurmountable difficulty. All I can say is that the frescoists of the past were not too much worried by it and painters to-day seem to have an equal dexterity. The thing is, never mix with the idea of matching what is painted but rather the image which one had when the first mixture was made, while remembering the quantity of each color which went into it and even the feel of the weight of that color on the knife when it was lifted from the glass. This sounds fantastic, but so is the process of maintaining equilibrium on a bicycle fantastic and yet a child can do it.

And what a training it is to get away from smudging about on a palette, adding a little of this or a little of that until one has no longer any idea of the quantities or even the colors themselves which went into a tone. One can mix colors for years in such a way and never understand the resources of a single pigment. In fresco, the painter comes to know the possibility of each color as a violinist knows his strings.

There are various ways of testing a tone, but none of them is as useful as your own instinct. The color can be put on a piece of semi-absorbent paper, like news-print paper, and dried. Another way is to put it on a lump of raw umber, where it dries immediately. But look out for the effect of the umber about it when judging your color, particularly if the natural tonality of your work is light and cool.

So always keep your colors liquid. Never give your plaster at one time more than it can absorb, for your tone will lose its resonance immediately. At the same time with a very full brush of liquid color you are forced to make a wash, yet in fresco such a wash is impossible unless it is an exceedingly pale tint. Whereon the loaded brush pauses an instant, the plaster greedily drinks all it can get and the result is inevitably spotty.

In my early experiments this problem worried me greatly. I could not see how to get the color on evenly and yet there were the old frescoes before my eyes without a trace of that spottiness. Then one day while I was thumbing over my beloved old "cook-book," as I call it, my Cennino Cennini, a phrase suddenly became significant to me. I had read the page a dozen times and was certain there was nothing on it which I had not studied, and yet there it was. "Squeeze the brush between your fingers." Try it. After a few days the causticity of the lime will make the skin peel from your hand; but this is of relatively little account and besides, you can wear a rubber glove on your left hand. You will find that even a squeezed brush will hold enough color for several long clear strokes—as much as an overloaded one would in water color. It is the moisture in the wall that makes this possible. What the plaster takes up unevenly from the brush is the surplus color. Once you have become accustomed to the ease of covering large spaces in fresco, you will forever after be impatient with the slow, painful method of applying the paint in every other medium.

This trick of painting with the squeezed brush accounts for the dragged look which the paint has in most of the fine old frescoes. The color has been drawn across the surface in the direction of the form; lengthwise, for instance, for an arm or a leg; in a circle about the eyes, and then spreading out so that it drops from the cheek bone to the chin. This is obvious in the early Byzantine work when the different tones are clearly demarcated, even emphasized, but the same principle applies to the great painting of the following period. It accounts in part for the solidity of form of the work of Giotto, for instance. If your structure is not absolutely logical this method will find you out. Spaces will be left which you literally cannot fill. And, as you are following the edge of the tone or value with the next, an incompletely understood form is sure to come to grief. The great cloak of a figure by Giotto holds together with the solidity and "inevitableness" of sculpture. The same, in a far more subtle way, is true of heads.

Another thing which gives the solidity in the old masters is the cool underpainting in monochrome which they invariably used. This was usually done in terra verde and emphasized with a darker tone called *verdaccio* composed of white, ochre, black and a touch of red.

Cennino gives in remarkable detail the ancient method of the underpainting and overpainting. His claim that it is the method of Giotto is not exaggerated, as a study of the master's work clearly shows. A close examination of the frescoes in the upper church at Assisi, when the light is excellent, has convinced me that it is textually Giotto's method.

I quote from Cennino (the translation is my own):

"Take the amount of a bean of dark ochre. There are two kinds, the light and the dark. If you haven't the dark, take the light, well ground. Put it in your glass and take the amount of a lentil of black and mix it with the ochre. Take a little bianco sangiovanni (prepared lime white) equal to a third of a bean, and a knife-tip of cinabrese (light red and lime white ground together). Mix these colors with the preceding and add enough clear water to make them runny and liquid—no tempera. Make a pigs' bristle brush of the size that will go into a goose quill and with this brush attack the head which you wish to do, always remembering that the face is divided into three parts: the forehead, the nose, and the chin, with the mouth. Sketch in your face little by little with your brush only slightly moistened with this color which in Florence is called verdaccio and in Sienna bazzeo. When you have formed it, if it seems to you out of scale or does not correspond with what you had planned, take your big bristle brush soaked with water and rub the plaster. Thus you can erase and correct.*

"Then have a little terra verde, very liquid, in another glass, and with your soft bristle brush held between the thumb and first finger of the left hand begin to shade under the chin and in all the darkest parts, passing again and again under the chin and in the corners of the mouth, under the nose, at the side under the lashes and perhaps at the side of the nose, a little about the ends of the eyes and about the ears. Thus with sentiment keep passing the color on the face and hands wherever the flesh tone is to go. Then with a pointed squirrel brush,

* *Author's Note:* This is an unwise proceeding as it takes away from the beauty of the surface. The use of the cartoon should make such erasures unnecessary.

pick out each contour, the nose, the eyes, the lips, the ears, with this same verdaccio.

"Nowadays there are masters who, when the face is in this state, take a little bianco sangiovanni mixed with water and establish the high lights and reliefs of the face in the desired order, then put a little red on the lips and the cheeks, and then finally with a little light wash that is very liquid flesh color, they go over the whole and the face is painted. They also touch up the reliefs again with a little white. This method is not bad. Others first cover the face with the local color of flesh and then model with a little verdaccio and flesh color, retouch with white, and the work is finished. These methods are those of people who know little. Believe me that what I am about to explain to you concerning the art of coloring is the veritable manner, since Giotto, the great master, considered it good enough for him.

"He had as a pupil Taddeo Gaddi, the Florentine, for twenty-four years. He was his godson. Taddeo's son was Agnolo and the latter had me with him for twelve years and he taught me this method with which he, Agnolo, could color in a manner even more mysterious and fresh than could Taddeo his father.

"First take a glass; put in it a small quantity of bianco sangiovanni and light cinabrese, equal parts, and with clean water make the mixture liquid. With your brush of soft bristles, well held between the fingers as above, go over the face which you have left sketched in with the terra verde. Pass this rosy color over the lips and the cheek bones. My master placed the rose of the cheeks more towards the ears than the nose because this adds to the modeling of the face. Soften this well into the tones about. Then have three glasses in which mix three different flesh tones; that is, the darkest (half again as light as your rosy color) and the two others lighter by degrees. Now take the glass of your lightest tint and with your soft bristle brush take of this flesh color, squeeze the brush between your fingers and pick out the reliefs of your face. Then take the glass of the next color and with it cover the middle tone of the face and hands as well as the feet and body when you are making a nude figure. Now take the glass of the third tint and go towards the edges of the shadows, stopping when the mixture would take away the value of the terra verde. In this manner come back several times, blending each tone with the other until all is well covered and as far as the nature of the subject suggests. But above all, avoid, if you want your work to shine by its freshness, letting your brush leave its place and go over the other flesh tones, unless it is to blend them skillfully and with art. Work and practice will make you more adept than books can possibly do. When you have passed these flesh tones, make another lighter, almost white, and with it touch the eyelids, the reliefs of the nose, the point of the chin, the edge of the ears. Then with a dry squirrel brush and pure white make the whites of the eyes, the tip of the nose and a touch on the edge of the mouth. Make these reliefs with delicacy. Put a little black in another glass and with the same brush draw the edge of the eye above the luminous part and from the nostrils and the openings of the ears. Now put a little dark sinopia in another glass and with it draw the lower line of the eyes, the contour of the nose, the eyelids, the mouth, and shade the underpart of the upper lip which should be a little darker than the lower. Before profiling these contours, take the same brush and the verdaccio to touch up the hair. With the same brush and white do the lights of the hair. Then with a wash of light ochre and a soft brush glaze all the hair as you did the flesh. Then with the same brush and dark ochre touch up the extremities. Then with a very fine pointed brush of squirrel, make the high lights of the hair with light ochre and bianco sangiovanni. Then with dark sinopia, profile the contours and edges of the hair as you did for the face.

"This is enough for a young face."

This passage needs no comment. It is impossible to write in more detail or with greater clarity.

Cennino was probably not a good painter. Such an all-absorbing interest in technique usually goes with a non-creative mind. No authoritative painting by him exists to-day. He must, however, have had a hand in many of Agnolo Gaddi's decorations and from the latter's work we can judge his method. It is that of Giotto but without the "delicacy" and "sentiment" which Cennino advises us to employ. The difference is in the use of the verdaccio. In Giotto it is very light and hardly distinguishable from the terra verde; in Agnolo it is dark and emphasized by a sharp outline.

The modern artist will find many other methods of painting in fresco. I have made countless experiments but in the end have come back to the basic principle of Cennino's system; that is, the cool underpainting in terra verde pure, building up the form by passing this wash again and again and then coming back later with the varied flesh tones, very liquid and repeated over and over. This system is inherent in the very nature of fresco, for in this medium certain methods of painting must be used at certain moments of the day and no other. In the morning the color must be very liquid to avoid choking the pores of the plaster. Towards evening it must also be liquid because the ground absorbs less and a thick coat tends to become too opaque in drying. The heaviest painting must be done during the middle of the day and the later hours kept for building up the accents and reliefs and glazing whenever necessary.

Herein lies the great fascination of fresco. Instead of the

dead and sometimes discouragingly inanimate surface of a canvas, you are struggling with a living thing. Your plaster, born so to speak in the morning, must have lived its life before night. Every instant it has its requirements and at moments when time grows short, its desperate needs. The tendency to work by the watch should make it the most modern of mediums. But for the artist it has the greatest quality of all—it forces him into a state of passionate absorption in which he must be utterly oblivious of everything but his work.

Although the painter's direct contact with the living thing in his plaster finishes with the day, that life continues to express itself actively for some time after. The drying change usually begins the following day. Years of experience will not make you entirely immune to worries which this change causes. The different colors dry at different speeds. Those mixed with much white sometimes stand out too much even towards the end of the day's work. Behind the colors the plaster is changing from grey to white. The result is a kind of measles which will tax your patience and self-confidence to the limit. After about a week your tones will have come back into harmony. Then begins the slow second drying process which may last six months or a year. It is almost impossible to describe, although it is familiar to everyone who has painted in fresco. During the period, the colors pull together, grow more restrained and at the same time more resonant, become little by little more harmoniously and mysteriously mural.

From then on, unlike oil painting which grows dark and dingy, fresco through the centuries becomes paler, more elusive and always more enchanting.

Chapter VIII

RETOUCHING

THERE really should be no retouching in fresco. It is a practice which should never be resorted to outdoors, as there is no medium for retouching which will withstand the action of rain and sun. Occasionally its use is justified indoors in order to correct some minor detail which mars an otherwise good piece or to repair damage done to the painting as sometimes happens while the plaster is still soft, particularly when there are workmen in the building. The best way to retouch in fresco is to destroy the piece by scraping it off and begin again. As one must usually, because of the progression of the work, repaint the same piece on the following day, several days' return to the same subject has a singularly salutary effect, and the tendency to make errors through being insufficiently prepared is remarkably reduced.

However, the old masters practiced retouching in tempera extensively. This is particularly true of the minor men. Cennino, who was one himself, gives a whole list of methods whereby passages left unfinished in the fresco were to be completed in secco.

This came in part from the fact that the blues were regularly painted in tempera. They believed that ultramarine —powdered lapis lazuli—had a poor adherence in fresco, and as the color was very valuable even in those days, it was the common practice to add the blues in secco. This was also true of certain other colors which could not be used on the fresh plaster, such as the lake red and quicksilver vermilion.

They ordinarily used the yolk of an egg with about the same quantity of water to make it fluid and added to this the color which itself was already ground in water. A little more water can still be safely added to this mixture.

The colors to be used with it are the same as in fresco, and with these can be used other good colors which are considered permanent in other media. But the lime white of fresco must always be replaced by flake or zinc white, ground, of course, in water.

This is the standard tempera and is still the best to-day. It can be replaced by the white and yolk used together or even by the white alone. The difficulty with these is their tendency to stringiness. In the case of the white alone, this is evercome by beating it into a froth and letting it drain for some hours. The fluid which results is easy to handle but one must be very careful not to use either too little, in which case it would not hold, or too much, which would result in bad cracks.

The reason for using the white alone is to get away from the yellow color of the yolk, although this color is almost imperceptible in the finished work.

Fra Angelico is believed to have used nothing but the white in his tempera painting and this accounts for the exquisite quality of his blues. He was, however, expert in this particular medium and knew and conquered all its difficulties.

The fresco painter who has only an occasional use for tempera for retouching would be wise to use the yolk alone.

Chapter IX

GOLD

THE Italian painters of the Renaissance often depended on gold ornament for an important part of their effect. This yellow metal was added when the plaster was dry; that is, some weeks after the fresco painting was completed at about the same time that the lapis blue was being applied in secco. The two, in fact, were usually considered together, partly because they were applied at the same time and partly because they were more precious than the other materials.

The gold is gold leaf. Pure 24-carat gold is beaten between sheets of vellum until it is a thin but still unbroken tissue. The modern beaters reduce it until it is far thinner than did those of the Renaissance but the effect is still about the same. This gold can be easily procured to-day and the expense is not prohibitive.

Wherever it is to be applied on the fresco, the suction of the ground must first be stopped. This is commonly done by giving the passages to be gilded one or two coats of spirit varnish, known as French lacquer. Over this the gold size is painted. This can be bought at color shops or the stores which sell gilders' supplies. It comes ready prepared and is made from linseed oil very much reduced by boiling. It is best to get the eighteen to twenty-four hour kind. This means that one must wait twenty-four hours from the time the size is applied before laying the gold. Usually this size is put on in the evening and is ready to receive the gold during the following day, in the morning or later according to the atmospheric condition.

It is better not to use the various quick-drying sizes except in repair work as, because of their rapidity of drying, there is only a short time during which they are in proper condition to hold the gold. However, for retouching, the twelve hour and even the half hour size, principally Japan varnish, is useful. I have also used French lacquer and even fine gelatine dissolved in water for retouching in spots when the thickness of gold size would be visible.

But for all permanent work the twenty-four hour variety is the best. It usually comes tinted with yellow ochre or chrome yellow in order to give the color of the gold, which is translucent, more substance. These colors may also be added to clear size.

It must be painted on with great care to see that it does not pass beyond the spaces to be gilded. It is best to use a small bristle brush and to spread it thinly to avoid a tendency to run.

The next day touch the size from time to time with your finger and when it is no longer moist but tacky, that is, when your finger sticks to it but remains clean, then it is ready for gilding. It will remain in this state for many hours.

Gold leaf, known as "patent gold", can be bought to-day in which each leaf has been attached to a sheet of tissue paper. This may be cut to the desired size with scissors, the leaf side applied to the size, the tissue side pressed with the fingers or with a soft, square-ended stencil brush, and the tissue lifted off leaving the gold attached to the tacky size. When the latter is quite dry, after forty-eight hours or more, the loose gold is dusted off with a very soft brush of the water color type and the work finished.

This "patent gold" is good for beginners and very useful for outside work when there is a breeze. But the old method is still the best, and its use is necessary in gilding uneven surfaces such as raised ornaments.

The standard gold comes in a booklet between each two sheets of which is a leaf of gold. The leaves are either taken out one by one by laying a gilder's knife across them and blowing gently to bend the leaf over the knife edge or, as the Italians do, the whole booklet is dumped out in a crumpled heap on one end of a gilder's cushion. This cushion is a small board slightly larger than a brick, padded and covered with chamois skin. It usually has a screen of stiff vellum around three sides to keep off the wind, as the slightest breath of air will send the gold flying.

A leaf is then picked up by the knife and laid flat on the free end of the cushion. It is then cut with the straight steel edge of the knife into halves, quarters, and at times even such small divisions as twenty-fourths. It is a mistake to try to handle too large a piece at a time. Even for a flat ground the half leaf is the easiest to manage. This cutting is done by a quick, firm, sawing motion, flat across the leaf.

The cut piece is then picked up by the "palette." This palette is a comb-like brush of badger the width of the gold leaf, with the bristles laid side by side. The palette is passed over the hair to make it slightly greasy—the Latin sometimes has an advantage over the Nordic in this—and the tips of the badger bristles touched to the edge of the gold. This makes the leaf adhere and it can be picked up and laid against the size where it immediately adheres. It should then be pressed gently with the soft water-color brush and in two or three days dusted and lightly polished with the same brush.

Note that it is the greasiness of the palette which makes the gold adhere. Consequently never touch it with your hands and do not touch the blade of the knife, as both oiliness and moisture will make the leaf attach itself and you will be hopelessly entangled. The knife can be kept clean by rubbing it with a sheet of the booklet which contained the gold. These booklets are coated with Armenian Bole, an oil and water repelling clay substance.

The gold is usually protected with a coat of French lacquer and alcohol in equal parts, which should only be applied after the size is thoroughly dry. Do not be worried when you see the lacquer grow cloudy, as it will become clear again in a few minutes.

This same process is used for silver and aluminum leaf. The size, however, must be uncolored and in the case of silver, the lacquering must be done as soon as possible as the metal oxidizes rapidly.

Renaissance fresco painters made a great deal of use of raised and tooled gold ornament. This is particularly true of Benozzo Gozzoli, Fra Angelico, Ghirlandaio and Signorelli. The raised halos were built up with a trowel or small tool in the fresh plaster immediately after the piece of the day was laid. Lime was then tooled into them with a steel or boxwood point. Designs were also pressed into them with stamps made of metal or hard wood. I had a set of stamps cut in Florence of bronze from my own designs.

This ornamentation has its practical use. Gold, because of its reflecting surface, has a range of values leading almost from white to black. This is often noticeable in photographs. By breaking up the surface, the reflection is diffused and a true yellow tone results.

The old masters also painted designs and elaborate brocades over gold. After the lacquering, any color may be superimposed in tempera, either in flat tones or in hatching.

One of the most charming touches in the old frescoes is the fine hair line gold ornament done directly over the frescoes. To make this possible, the suction has to be stopped over the entire area in which these lines are to go, as otherwise the size will spread and become mat.

To accomplish this, when the fresco is dry a sponge is passed over the parts to be ornamented, saturated with the yolk and white of an egg mixed with a small bowlful of water. This is sufficient to stop the suction and is invisible to the eye. The size is then painted on with a very fine camel's hair brush, allowed to become tacky, and the gilding proceeds as usual, only with faintly divided leaves. After the surplus metal is dusted off, the original fine line remains with all its charm.

Gold for grounds or ornament is not in common use to-day, although properly employed it has a noble and monumental character. Its use as a supplementary color is closely associated with the art and history of fresco painting. It is a pity that more experiments are not made with it in a manner other than archaic.

Chapter X

REMOVING AND RE-LOCATING FRESCOES

"WONDERS are many in the world, and the wonder of all is man," wrote Sophocles; and went on to cite instances of human ingenuity and resourcefulness. He would have been lost in admiration, surely, if he could have witnessed the operation by which fresco paintings are actually removed from the walls upon which they were executed, and re-located in other situations.

At first thought it must seem to the layman that such an achievement must be rather more than next to impossible. A layer of paint is a pretty thin and fragile thing. One can think of it being scraped off a surface, and destroyed in the scraping, but how could it be lifted off intact? Moreover, a fresco painting is not merely a layer of paint on plaster — it is part of the plaster itself, it can never be removed from the plaster except by the process of destruction. As to removing the whole *intonaco,* as the Italians called the built-up thickness of plaster prepared for the fresco colors, it seems obvious that it would respond to such a preposterous attempt by promptly crumbling to dust. Nevertheless, the thing is done. Human ingenuity found a way. In fact, it is very simple.

For enlightenment on the technique of this modern miracle the writer is indebted to one who is widely considered the greatest living master of fresco, the Mexican artist José Clemente Orozco.

Señor Orozco's first advice about removing frescoes was, to be sure, identical with Punch's advice about getting married — "Don't." A fresco, he pointed out, is more than a part of the plaster — it is a part of the wall, the building, the situation for which it was designed. If it was executed by an artist worthy of the name, a fresco is a work which holds its full significance, and reveals its full beauty, only in the structure it was meant to adorn, in the space it was made to fill, under the light and shadow which conditioned the artist's original conception. All that is certainly true. Nevertheless, Time has its way with frescoes as with every mortal work. The tooth of dampness may take centuries to gnaw a wall, yet it will make its mark in the end. Or a wall built as they built of old may stand while a world changes, yet at last give warning that it too is to share the fate of all things mortal. Progress may require as part of its price the razing of a church, a monastery, a palace where centuries ago the dream of an artist took form. In short, though frescoes should not be removed from their original sites, sometimes frescoes have to be removed, or abandoned to destruction.

And so this problem of the transit of an actual section of a solid wall to a new site is solved by calling on the aid of insubstantial paper and glue. The surface of the fresco to be moved is first covered with sheets of fine thin paper, which is made to adhere to the plaster by the use of a water-soluble glue. Over the first layer of paper another layer is glued; over that another; and so on until there has been built up a panel, consisting of layers of paper glued together, thick enough and staunch enough to support the weight of the plaster-layer, the *intonaco,* which is to be removed. A thicker paper-and-glue panel will be built up for a large and heavy job than for a small one; thickness of an inch or more is sometimes required. After the first few layers, the paper used should be thicker and tougher, and of course need not be so fine. The glue must always be easily soluble in water.

Now you have a staunch, stiff panel to which the *intonaco,* stained by the precious pigments, can safely cling while being transported across the street or around the world—provided you can get the said *intonaco* to relinquish its grip upon the wall that has been, perhaps for centuries, its solid fundament and material anchor. This is a simpler matter than devising the paper-and-glue panel, but a much harder matter to execute. First of course the depth of the *intonaco* must be ascertained by boring. Then all that is done is to chisel this *intonaco,* this layer of plaster, loose from the wall, chiselling under it all the way; in essence a simple operation, in execution one requiring care and delicacy. But when at last the whole layer of plaster is loosened, it may easily be lifted from that site where the artist trowelled it on and stained it with his colors, and go forth to its new destiny, absurdly but safely clinging to a panel of paper and glue.

The new site for a removed fresco must be prepared, of course, as the original wall was prepared. It should be a dry wall and free from saltpetre if the fresco's new life is not to turn quickly to death. It should be sturdy, as all walls should be; the inner surface must be roughened, or prepared with a mortar containing rubble or fragments of stone and brick, or this inner surface may consist of tile or of wire lath. Against this inner surface of the wall, properly moistened, the *intonaco* is laid and gently pressed and held in position until it has gripped the new wall as it gripped the old.

And then the paper-and-glue panel is removed from the surface; the outer layers torn away; the inner layers lifted as the glue dissolves, carefully and patiently. Chemistry serves man in one of the simplest ways: the glue yields utterly to water, the fresco utterly rebuffs water; and presently whatever of beauty the transplanted picture has for the world, shines out as radiantly from its new site as from its old, none the worse for its strange experience and its strange journey.

In the museum, *Del Parque,* in Barcelona, there are many Romanic frescoes taken from churches in the Catalonian hills. The way in which these frescoes were removed, according to Professor José Pijoan, was after an Italian technique as follows:

First, the fresco was marked off into small divisions which could be easily reassembled. These divisions were then removed one by one in the following manner: Blotting paper was pasted on the frescoes with a substance soluble in water. A second blotter was pasted over the first, and over the second was glued a piece of canvas. Over the latter was placed a very thin coating of plaster of Paris. The *intonaco* with its blotting paper and canvas coverings and about one-half inch of the plaster surface was cut away from the wall, and while it was being removed, was rolled up as an ordinary canvas. The perfect condition of these reassembled frescoes in the Barcelona museum demonstrates that the process is a sound one.

9. GARDNER HALE (1894-1931). *Portraits of the Count and Countess d'Hinnisdal and Their Four Daughters. (detail) From the fresco in the church at Souvrain Moulin, France.*

10. GARDNER HALE.
From the fresco in the house of J. S. Carlisle at Islip, L. I. Painted in 1917.

11. GARDNER HALE. *Descent from the Cross.*
From the fresco in the Chapel at Pau, France.

12. JOSÉ CLEMENTE OROZCO (1883-1949). *Prometheus. (detail)*
From the fresco in Frary Hall, Pomona College, Claremont, California. Courtesy of the Delphic Studios, New York.

Chapter XI

THE PLACE OF FRESCO IN THE HISTORY OF PAINTING

PLATO banned the poets from his ideal Republic, but seems to have made no objection to sculptors and painters; for, being what a certain modern writer called a "word-fellow," he knew the disturbing and revolutionary power of poetry, but did not suspect that the chisel and the brush also mold and modify civilizations and men's concepts of life and eternity. Yet, without awakening the old and happily sleeping controversy as to whether analogies can usefully be drawn between the arts, or one interpreted in terms of another, we can with assurance assert that all the arts have a common origin.

There will never, fortunately, be a final answer to the eternal question, "What is Art?"' but the more fundamental question, "Why are the Arts?" is susceptible of a simple answer. Man is ever face to face with wonders and beauties comprehended and mysteries incomprehensible; and it is in response to a need rooted in the soul, to testify to these wonders and beauties, and to grapple with these mysteries, that certain individuals are endowed with the power to state, symbolize and interpret them to all men's eyes and ears. Millennia before man attained to civilization, he felt the compulsion to chant not only the story of his prowess in chase and combat, but also the wonder, terror and ecstasy of life and the world; and not long after the first poet sang, it would seem, the first draughtsman drew, nor was it a much later day when the first painter painted.

A sharp stick, an edged flint, served the primitive artist to make sketches. But materials for painting lay ready to his hand—soft stones that would leave red, or yellow, or brown marks on the grey flanks of the rocks—colored earth that furnished a ready and extensive, if crude, palette. The paintings in the caves of Altamira, in Spain, are attributed to paleolithic man. The hands that made them have been dust, twice ten thousand years. Painting is a very old art. And since paleolithic man lived principally in caves, mural painting was probably the first branch of the art practised, as it is the oldest of which examples survive.

It is of course true that, despite the incurably careless use of the word by writers who know better, the masterly pictures of Altamira and other timeless cave-paintings are not frescoes. But it also appears to be true that fresco painting is of an antiquity really amazing when one considers the ingenuity and inventiveness that went to the elaborating of its technique, simple though that is in its essence. Come forward a few thousand years from paleolithic times to the prehistoric period in Egypt; Flinders Petrie tells us that this extended from about 8000 to about 5800 B.C.; and already we find fresco known and used for limning on the walls of tombs the story of mortal deeds and the gods' assessments of the soul.

In Egypt, in fact, fresco would seem to have been distinctly the primitive medium; for if it was used at all in later years, it was overshadowed by other media. The Egyptians painted not only tombs, but inner and outer wall surfaces of temples and palaces, and statues as well. All of these required to be covered with plaster as a basis for the application of colors. Nevertheless the early-discovered fresco medium was abandoned, and the colors were put on perishably with gum, glue, and in Roman times with wax and probably with egg. Reasons for these developments are not far to seek. The acacia grows abundantly in Egypt, and this tree is the source of gum arabic, the medium for water color painting; and this medium came to be used extensively for painting upon papyrus. Now in the warm, dry air of the Nilotic empire, the moisture-resistant qualities of fresco were not needed; water-soluble media were quite feasible for mural work; so the simpler technique developed for painting on the papyrus was transferred to wall-pictures and pictures in tombs. Egyptian paintings which, escaping violence, had survived not merely centuries but millennia, have been proved to be water colors by the simple means of removing the pigment with a wet finger. The use of tempera, the egg medium, in Egypt, is a supposition; the use of encaustic, the wax medium, at least in the late or Roman period, is proved by surviving examples.

If we can forget paleolithic times and such dates as 8000 and 5800 B.C., we can reasonably concede a respectable antiquity to the next verified examples of true fresco painting—those discovered adorning the walls of the palace of Knossos in Crete. It is not surprising that the ancient Cretans, the rediscovery of whose forgotten civilization has so profoundly affected our concepts of historical and cultural development, should have hit upon the secret of the most enduring of media; though indeed they may have got it from Egypt, for analysis of the Knossian frescoes discloses the presence of the pigment known as Egyptian frit, proving the existence of commerce between Egypt and Crete at least as early as 1500 B.C., the date assigned to these murals.

Dates are not so easily given for Etruscan remains, but among them too we find true frescoes. It is exciting to think that the medium later to be so gloriously associated with the name and fame of Italian art, had root in Italian soil centuries before the Christian era. It would be pleasant to believe that on that soil it never quite died out; but the belief would apparently be no more than a fancy.

The writers of the Renaissance, as we see to-day, deplorably muddled cultural history by their manner of using the terms "the ancients" and "the ancient times." Blandly telescoping a millennium and a half, they spoke of that vast span of time between the day when blind Homer sung and the day when Rome fell, as one era; though in those fifteen centuries not only such outer things as empires, but such inner things as cultures, rose and fell. This egregious habit—with the general substitution of the term "classic" in place of "ancient"—has been continued by French and English scholars in particular, until only to-day history, in alliance with archaeology and other sciences that have no reverence for "classical concepts," is making it ridiculous. It is no matter for wonder, therefore, that it is still a matter of dispute whether true fresco was or was not known and practised in "classical times." As a matter of fact, it would appear that it was and it wasn't.

No testimony on the point has come to us from ancient Greece; but from the days of imperial Rome we have the writings of Pliny the Elder and Vitruvius. These are to the modern understanding not a little ambiguous; which circumstance has added greatly to the delights of controversy among commentators since the dawn of the Revival of Learning, but has not helped much toward a solution of the vexed question, whether true fresco was or was not practised in the Graeco-Roman world during the Athenian, Hellenic and Imperial eras. The directions of Vitruvius for preparing walls to receive colors are merely incidental to a book on architecture. As to Pliny the Elder, he was a gossip and a potterer—a dilettante. In the intervals of luxurious living he jotted down impartially facts which came under his own observation—none too accurate—and fables and superstitions more worthy of a peasant or heathen than of a Roman patrician. The character of this Pliny is summed up in the circumstances of his death. Lively, undiscriminating curiosity he had: wherefore he went personally to investigate the disaster which overwhelmed Pompeii and Herculaneum; but he perished on the shore from heat and suffocation while attempting to return to his ship; for he was fat—he had lost his physical resilience, and with it, plainly enough, his mental clarity.

Pliny's many references to painting, therefore, tease us and puzzle us more than they enlighten. He tells us that encaustic was unsuitable to the painting of walls, yet mentions instances of its use for that purpose, without indicating whether the instances he cites were exceptional. He enlarges at some length on painting with wax by two distinct methods; but so ineptly that until Flinders Petrie unearthed examples of both methods from Egyptian ruins of the Roman period, we could not be sure of his meaning or that he really knew what he was writing about. He ascribes to one Ludius the invention, in Rome, of a method of painting "on uncovered places in maritime cities" (as Guevara paraphrases him) "with little expense, and in a most agreeable manner," but the passage so lacks clarity that many commentators consider that he was referring to distemper painting, and not to fresco. In other places, however, he refers specifically to fresco, as when he says that the pigment known as melinum, which came from Melos, could not be used in this kind of painting; and when he tells us that Panaeus the brother of Phidias covered the walls of the temple of Minerva at Elis with lime and marble, mixed with milk and saffron (for milk apparently was much used at various periods, and its use, with water, would not deprive the medium of the name of fresco; while from another passage in Pliny it appears that the saffron was added merely to give the pictures a pleasant scent—a rather charming sensual refinement). Pliny also tells of pictures in Ardea and Lanuvium which, unprotected by roofs and exposed to the elements, had endured many years without deterioration; these passages are considered among the strongest proofs that fresco was practised in Italy before the days when Pliny wrote, but it is characteristic of the old potterer that he neglected to note the specific fact.

Pliny's pages contain many notes concerning pigments, and these passages have value; though the discrimination necessary in reading them is sufficiently indicated by the fact that he supposes dragon's blood to be literally the blood of dragons, and even gives a detailed account of the gory combats in which elephants and dragons bring each other to mutual death, thus enabling this sanguinary pigment to be secured. Pliny also discourses on the preparation of the plaster or stucco base for mural painting, especially praising that made with three sand coats and two coats of marble dust—which latter was certainly much in favor in ancient time, particularly because it could be brought to a very high and bright polish. The passages in Vitruvius pertinent to our subject are also largely concerned with the composition and application of the mortar and plaster foundation for painting on walls.

In the valuable modern book, *Greek and Roman Methods of Painting,* by A. P. Laurie, M.A., D.Sc., there are passages dealing with the directions of Vitruvius, which I cannot do better than quote:

"In the seventh book of his work on Architecture, after describing the making of concrete floors and the preparation of lime, and the plastering of arches and cornices, he [Vitruvius] proceeds as follows, in the middle of the third chapter:

When the cornices are finished, the walls are to be trowelled as roughly as possible, and thereafter, when the trowelling is somewhat dry, over it the directions of the sand-mortar are to be so traced out, that in length it must be true by the rule, in height by the plumb-line, and the angles by the square. For thus the surface of the plaster will be faultless for pictures. When this (first coat) is slightly dry, a second is to be laid on, and then a third. The firmer and sounder the laying on of the sand-mortar, the more solid and durable will the plaster-work be. When besides the trowelling not less than three coats of sand have been set out, applications of marble-dust are to be used. This stuff is to be so tempered that in the spreading it does not stick to the trowel, but the iron comes out of the mortar clean. A coat of marble-dust having been laid on and getting dry, another rather thin coat is to be applied. When this has been beaten and well rubbed, another still finer is to be put on. Thus with three coats of sand and as many of marble, the walls are so firm that they cannot crack or become defective in any way. And, moreover, solidity being secured by rubbing with planes, and smoothness from the hardness and sheen of the marble, the walls will give out with great brilliance colours applied with polishings. For colours, when they are carefully laid on damp plaster, do not get loose, but are forever permanent, for this reason, that the lime, losing all its moisture in the kiln, is so dry and porous that it readily imbibes whatever chances to touch it, and solidification taking place from the mixtures of the various potentialities whose elements or first principles are brought together, the resulting substance, of whatever it is composed, when it becomes dry, is such that it seems to have special qualities peculiar to itself. Thus plaster-work which is well executed neither becomes rough from age nor when it is washed does it give up the colours unless they have been laid on carelessly and on a dry surface. . . .

"We shall now consider" (writes Laurie) "the information to be derived from this passage." He notes that "the instructions for preparing the plaster surface are perfectly clear and definite," and that the passage plainly contains directions for laying pigments on wet lime. He continues:

"There is a most interesting attempt to explain the way in which the lime and pigments ultimately form a homogeneous whole. If, instead of speaking of the lime losing its moisture, Vitruvius had said losing its carbonic acid, the passage with this emendation might have been written by a modern chemist describing the scientific basis of buon fresco. . . .

"In the next place, it is to be noted that Vitruvius does not speak of this as the *only* method of wall-painting, but as the most *durable* method, and contrasts it with the results obtained by painting on a dry surface.

"We have here definite evidence that painting on dry walls was also customary, in which case some medium like glue would doubtless be used, and this goes a long way to explain the conflicting conclusions of investigators and chemists.

"Vitruvius in effect tells us that he is familiar with painting on dry walls, necessarily with some binding medium, and with painting on wet lime, and he regards the wet lime painting as the more permanent. He would not have come to this conclusion without a wide experience of both methods. . . ."

Understood as Laurie understands them, these passages from Vitruvius would seem to prove sufficiently the practise of true fresco in the Rome of Augustus. In fact, I am inclined to understand these remarks as referring to fresco only; for the words "nor when it is washed does it give up the colours unless they have been laid on carelessly and on a dry surface" I would take to be in the nature of admonition against careless workmanship and reproof for careless workmen who let the plaster, intended for fresco, get dry. Nevertheless we shall see that some commentators urge cogent arguments against the supposition that Vitruvius was referring to fresco at all; so that here also we are baffled in our quest for a definite answer to the question, whether buon fresco was known to the Athenian, Hellenic and Roman worlds.

Vasari says summarily, "Fresco painting was much in use among the ancients." Two centuries later, Vincenzo Requeno, in his *Saggi sul ristablimento dell' antica arte de' Greci e Romani pittori* (Venice, 1784) argued at length that "the ancients" did not paint in buon fresco. "In the work of Vitruvius," he says, "there is no mention made of painting, as is generally believed, but only of the preparation of the *intonaco* for painting. . . . The words of Vitruvius, 'colores udo tectorio cum diligenter sunt indacum, &c.' (when the colours are carefully laid on the wet plaster), must undoubtedly be understood of the various colours with which the *intonachi,* while still wet, were stained. Then that the preparation of the *intonaco* for painting on, of which alone Vitruvius speaks in this chapter, formerly included the operation of colouring the *intonaco,* before it was dry, with red or yellow, or with some other colour, which, besides what Vitruvius tells us in this third chapter of his *De tectoris operibus,* is proved by the ancient pictures of Herculaneum. When, by any accident, the colours of these scale off, the uniform colour of the ground beneath the elegant figure with which they are painted is seen. As authorities, I cite Winckelmann, and the academicians of Herculaneum, who, observing that when some of the pictures were cleaned with water, all the colours of the figures washed off, and there remained a ground, uniform in colour, smooth, fair, and polished, upon the ancient walls, concluded that the pictures of Herculaneum were painted by the Romans, in *secco,* upon an *intonaco,* stained in fresco." Signor Requeno develops this argument at great length, and a bit repetitively. He makes a telling point by citing from another page of Vitruvius, directions to mix glue and white lead with colors to be laid upon the stained *intonachi;* "all which things," he says, "are incompatible with true fresco painting." Therefore if we are to agree with Signor Requeno, any structure of confidence in ancient Greek and Roman practise of true fresco, resting on the evidence of Vitruvius, must tumble like a house of cards. The learned Pablo de Cespedes (born at Cordova in 1538, died in 1608, and himself a master of fresco) reports that in his time the painters of Rome contended that the ancients did not practise true fresco.

He, however, cited the old pictures found in Roman grottoes and subterranean vaults as proof that fresco was known in those remote times; but he hastens to note, "it is objected, that these are evidently not fresco, but distemper painting;" and he concludes, "although I have seen several, I cannot tell which they are, though I rather think they are frescoes, and the state they are in is not sufficiently perfect to enable me to decide." Señor Pablo was an honest man, not one to make up his mind hastily that what he wished to be so, was so! But in the end he inclines toward belief in ancient fresco practise, for he cites the fact that the paintings in the Temple of Public Safety in Rome, executed by Fabius Pictor, lasted three hundred years, until they were destroyed by fire in the reign of the Emperor Claudius. Francisco Pacheco, another Spanish frescoist who also wrote about the art, agrees with the final conclusions of de Cespedes, and argues that "all that is not oil painting, must necessarily be distemper, and, in reality, fresco is a particular kind of distemper," and considers this a reply to "those who wish to make it appear that the ancients painted in distemper only." Pacheco adds, "It cannot be denied that the ancients painted in fresco, from the duration of their paintings." Duration is certainly always a good argument for fresco, but of course Señor Pacheco did not know that Egyptian pictures would be dug up three centuries later which, after enduring for thousands of years, would rub off under a wet finger. To return for a moment to Requeno's argument, the fact that in the Augustan age the plaster prepared for painting, the *intonaco,* was stained while wet, does not seem to me to dispose conclusively of the supposition that Vitruvius may have been giving directions for painting the picture as well as staining the *intonaco.*

Moreover, it would appear that further examination of the pictorial remains of Pompeii and Herculaneum casts doubt on the conclusions which Requeno reached in the eighteenth century; for Laurie, commenting that the results of analysis are not conclusive as to the nature of these pictures — in some cases no binding vehicle for the pigments being found, in other cases such a vehicle apparently being present, and the vehicle in some cases being, apparently, egg or glue, which would be inconsistent with fresco, and in other cases milk, which might not be so inconsistent — notes that "on the whole the evidence of the experts is in favour of the conclusion that in these cases we are dealing with buon fresco."

In jumping ahead to cite the opinions of Vasari, de Cespedes, Pacheco, Requeno and Laurie, we have neglected the good monk Theophilus. Of this worthy man we know only that he was also called Ruggiero; that he lived and wrote in some forgotten German monastery probably early in the thirteenth century, but possibly as early as the eleventh; and that he composed a book as admirable in its learning as it is touching in its piety, in three parts, which deal respectively with painting, glass-making and working in metals. The section on painting consists of forty chapters — but chapters in those days were often very brief — most of which are concerned with pigments and their preparation, the laying on of the colors, and the preparations of panels, the making of glue, and so forth. But chapter fifteen is of especial interest to us, because it contains directions for painting on walls.

Theophilus gives directions for unmistakable fresco painting. He directs that "when figures, or birds, or representations of other objects, are drawn on a dry wall, the wall must be immediately sprinkled with water until it is quite wet. And all the colours which are to be put on, must be mixed with lime, and laid on at one wetting, in order that they may dry along with the wall, and may adhere to it." But he also goes on to direct the laying of certain colors "tempered with the yolk of an egg mixed with plenty of waters." Mrs. Merrifield concludes from these passages of Theophilus that in his time, ceilings were painted in secco, while walls were begun in fresco and finished in distemper or secco.

But the problem posed by the manuscript of Theophilus is, whether it is more credible to suppose that it preserves, in its reference to fresco technique, a tradition that had lasted a thousand years since "ancient times;" or, that it proves the re-invention of that technique in the monasteries of the maligned "Dark Ages" two or three centuries before it became the glory of Italian painting under the brushes of Cimabue and his radiant successors?

Mrs. M. P. Merrifield, whose translation of Cennino Cennini was published in 1844, two years later published an equally useful book of translations from the principal known medieval, renaissance and early modern commentators on fresco painting—to which, in the early Victorian manner, she gave the formidable title, *The Art of Fresco Painting, as Practised by the Old Italian and Spanish Masters, with a Preliminary Inquiry into the Nature of the Colours used in Fresco Painting, with Observations and Notes.* In addition to Theophilus, Vasari, Cespedes and Pacheco, Mrs. Merrifield lists and offers samples of the writings of Cennino Cennini (1437), Leon Battista Alberti (1485), Don Felipe de Guevara (1550), Ridolfo Borghini (1584), Giovanni Battista Armenio (1587), Andrea Pozzo (1693), and Don Acisclo Antonio Palomino de Castro y Velasco (1715). The dates given are, at least approximately, the years of publication of the works quoted from.

These several treatises are largely concerned with inquiries concerning the pigments used by the ancients and the painters of the Renaissance, with directions and advice concerning various media, and, more to our purpose, with the preparation of the *intonachi,* or layers of mortar and plaster with which walls were covered preparatory to receiving paintings, both in fresco and in other media. It would fill a volume as large as this whole book if I were to attempt a digest of the varieties of information and advice given by these various scholars. They boil down, after all, to a general agreement on the principles of preparing the *intonachi,* and on the colors that are and are not suitable to this medium and that. Any one of these writers, of course, is apt to discover a strong devotion to some particular theory; thus Guevara rejects with some scorn the procedure of plastering each day only the piece to be finished that day; he demands that the whole wall shall be plastered at once, and then goes to some pains to devise ways to moisten such portion as is to be painted on any one occasion. Most of the writers cited also give more or less explicit directions for the preparation of cartoons, in which matter there was considerable divergence of practise through the centuries. A passage in Vasari concerning the use of cartoons has led to much speculation. He directs that after the subject has been traced from the cartoon upon the *arricciato,* or middle layer of plaster, it shall then be covered by the *intonaco,* using the word to mean the final, outer coat of plaster. It is not easy to see of what use the tracing on the *arricciato* would be as a guide to the final execution of the picture, once it was hidden under the opaque *intonaco!* An anonymous writer quoted by Mrs. Merrifield suggests that the first tracing on the *arricciato* was made for the purpose of estimating the merits and deficiencies of the design; after which a corrected cartoon was prepared, from which the final picture was executed after the application of the *intonaco.*

As might be supposed, in the full flood of late Italian painting, there were some artists so incredibly skilful that they could dispense with the use of cartoons and, attacking the wall direct, paint their pictures rapidly and unhesitatingly at the first onset. Lorenzo Garbieri did this; but when cautious patrons required him to make cartoons, he would copy these from the picture, having first completed the latter! We are not surprised to learn that Garbieri was at times vexatiously persecuted by less adept technicians, jealous of his uncanny skill. Cesare Baglione also painted without cartoons, and was a man of such self-confidence and wit that when jealous plodders attempted to discredit him with his patrons, he turned the joke on them. But doubtless the most astonishing of these magicians of the art was that one described by Vasari in this passage:

> Amico Aspertino painted with both hands at once, holding in one hand a brush filled with light colour, and in the other, one filled with dark; but what was more remarkable and laughable, was that he bound round his waist a leather strap, to which hung his gallipots of tempered colours; and he looked like the devil of San Maccario with all his phials hanging 'round him, and when painting with his spectacles on his nose, it was sufficient to make the very stones laugh, especially when he began to talk, for he talked enough for twenty persons, and he loved to say the strangest things in the world.

The practise of fresco painting, it is clear, has produced some robust characters, as well as some exalted, dreamy, poetic creators of loveliness!

We are not losing sight of the fact that neither in "ancient times," during the Renaissance, nor in the modern era, have all mural paintings been done in buon fresco. It is no part, however, of the plan and purpose of this book, to consider at any length the whole subject of mural painting; to which one volume or a dozen could easily be devoted. We have seen that in the Egypt of the Pharaohs, walls were decorated in water colors, and that later in the Egypt of the Ptolemies, probably both encaustic and tempera were used in mural decoration. Analysis of Greek wall paintings has shown the presence of an unidentified binding medium and also of wax; Laurie supposes that wax was much used for mural work in Greece, where a warm dry climate facilitated its application; but that in Italy its use was confined, for the most part, to the painting of panels.

The tempera medium was probably used for mural painting in Imperial Rome, and certainly in the "Dark Ages" and early Medieval times. Overshadowed as a mural medium by buon fresco from the time of Cimabue to the twilight of the Renaissance, it never fell wholly into disuse; and when the force of that great impulse which made the Italian Renaissance burst upon the world in glory, was spent, and the race of giants was succeeded in Italy and Spain by the tribe of merely good painters, craftsmen and copyists, men who did not measure up to the demands of buon fresco, tempera painting was still practised. But meanwhile from the North, from Germany and Flanders, the use of the oil medium had spread. In those lands it had already discovered masters. Italian and Spanish artists took to it; investigated it for its novelty, adopted it for its facility.

The use of tempera and oil for mural work of course implies the preparation of a gesso over the stone wall or the wood panelling forming the foundation. Doubtless during the ages many attempts have been made to paint directly upon an unprepared wall or uncoated panels, but Time has not spared such follies. In modern times an ill-begotten form of mural decoration has sometimes been practised, the painting being done on canvas, and the canvas stretched upon the wall. It is certain that the centuries to come will bring experiments and innovations also, nor can anyone attentive to the lessons of history suppose that there will not be, among these, discoveries of value. Only recently the American artist Boardman

Robinson executed some large murals in a Pittsburgh department store, using automobile paint, a medium with obvious qualities of brilliance, though like all media tried by men through the ages, it must endure the assay of Time.

Of course one could also fill a dozen volumes merely tracing the history of buon fresco since the days of Cimabue, enumerating the most notable examples of it adorning the walls of churches and palaces, public buildings and private homes, attempting some comparative estimates of merits, giving rein to enthusiasm over the works of the masters. And since such a survey would open so endless a prospect, it too falls without the scope of this book. I have in previous pages sufficiently noted my view of the rise and decline of buon fresco, and sufficiently recorded my enthusiasms and allegiances. Really to know the greatness of the great frescoes, one must make the prayerful pilgrimage of Italy and Spain. Our hasty glance at the centuries, the millennia, in these pages, serves to give us some idea of the place of buon fresco in the history of mural decoration and in the story of painting throughout the ages.

So that now we are perhaps prepared to turn our thoughts to generations and centuries yet unborn, and to speculate, not too idly, on the future of fresco painting.

Chapter XII

THE FUTURE OF FRESCO

THOSE men of older centuries whom we call wisest, made few predictions about the future; and doubtless in later times we shall be thought wiser in degree as we are wary and reticent of prophecy. Yet so good a general rule must be relaxed to afford indulgence for the enthusiast to forecast a coming state of glory for the particular art, science or study that engages his enthusiasm; for it is enthusiasm and faith that bring things to pass. So marked a revival of interest in fresco painting as these recent years have seen, after the art had been two or three centuries in desuetude, naturally excites high hope in the minds of its modern practitioners, and irresistibly invites to prophecy.

In the earlier pages of this book there are some passages glancing at the future; which, without asking the reader to turn back at this point, we may summarize. There it is boldly said that there is ground for believing that the future of fresco lies in America. One reason for this, it is pointed out, is that opportunities for monumental work are fewer in Europe—for Europe, very largely, is built; but America is building, and "everywhere there are bare walls which must be ornamented." To be sure, two great nations of Europe seem to have entered upon a very extensive course of re-building—Germany and Russia—and doubtless these too will presently bethink themselves of fresco as the crowning glory of great structural achievement; but in this matter young America has the head-start. There are, as mentioned above, many walls already erected but standing unfinished for want of adequate and fitting decoration; and even in the days of the great depression, which still shadows the land as these words are written, great structures, particularly those "sky-scrapers" that are America's most startling contribution to architecture, continue to rise. Assuredly the opportunity is here, in so far as great wall spaces constitute that opportunity, and in so far as that inner "wistful and yearning" quality detected in our business men is ready to pay tribute to the need of art. Moreover, if and when a distressed, bewildered and timid America becomes again the opulent, confident, proud and assertive America which we can remember but a few years back, one of the conditions historically associated with periods of rich and flourishing art-achievement will be present. It is certain, too, as indicated in the first chapter, that American painters, presently as competent in technique and as alert and authentic in the seeking spirit of the artist as any in the world, can readily rise to the opportunity to add the glories of buon fresco to our "bare walls." But are these things all that are needed?

Looking back, we see that the Italian and Spanish worlds in the days when the masterpieces of fresco were wrought, were rich and opulent worlds, and we draw the conclusion that riches and confidence and pride will also breed monumental art within these shores. But we overlook a factor of greater importance than the riches of Florence or the power of Rome: that factor was a living, stirring faith that gave the artists their inner power. Without such a faith to-day, can we produce an art that will be anything but surface?

The great present-day master of the fresco medium, Orozco, surely should have something to say on this point; and in fact he has. All of Orozco's achievements come from within. When the Mexican Ministry of Education gave him great wall-spaces to cover with the message of the Revolution, it also gave the same opportunity to other Mexican artists. But the others had been to Paris, and came back to advance their several favorite Parisian modes and theories. Orozco had stayed in Mexico. When he addressed himself to the blank walls before him, the things that took form were not pictures conceived according to the rules of this or that school, but vast, amazing, appalling, agonized, peremptory apparitions drawn from two sources: the things Orozco saw about him in war-torn, bleeding, suffering, triumphing Mexico, and the things Orozco, a soldier of the Revolution, felt within him to the last drop of his blood and the inner marrow of his bones. And it is the art of Orozco that has been named great.

"What is necessary for great fresco painting in future America? Why, the revolutionary feeling, the activity of the revolution," said Orozco.

"But we are not going to have revolution in the United States. Even under the pressure and hardship of these times, American thought takes no revolutionary turn. There is no revolutionary impulse in our people. We are rooted in an ordered past and a comparatively prosperous system. We are patient. However we work out our problem, it will not be by revolution. Is there then no future for great fresco work in the United States?"

"There is a future," said the Mexican. "I speak naturally of revolution, but I know the term is unsuitable to the problem in this country. I do not mean that you must have revolution in the sense of anarchical disorder. But you must have revolution in another deep and real sense. Perhaps the term 'renovation' will express what I mean. You must have a period of great activity, but not merely in money-making, in growing prosperous, in putting up great structures for the sake of show and advertisement and corporate pride. It must be a period of activity in thought, in ideas, bold, creative, new ideas.

"Otherwise you may cover a million walls in fresco, but it will all be merely dead copying of the past. What I mean is"—

the artist groped for verbal expression—"that painting on great walls, on the walls of public buildings, is not a matter of private amusement or the glorification of individuals or corporations; but such painting is a social function and must therefore be a social responsibility. And so the artist must have something to say, something of his own, yet something that his times and his people and his country are trying to say, something prophetic. . . ." José Clemente Orozco's resources in the English language failed him, but he had said enough to demand prayerful thought.

If Orozco is right, our prediction of a great future for fresco in America requires this modification: mere wall-space will not do; mere opulence, power and cockiness will not do; mere *fatness* will not do. These things may breed murals featuring Greek goddesses with Ziegfeld girl faces and no bodies that one can feel under politely classic draperies, clutching indifferently sheaves of wheat or locomotives, with cornucopias or automobiles indifferently tucked under their arms. Or these things may breed murals recording with fair fidelity the surfaces of modern life; or murals attempting to symbolize these times by stiff, unimaginative, puerile use of modern properties, cars and cranes and dynamos presided over by physical culture magazine men with collar-advertisement countenances. But only profound and excited feeling, only a sense of something to say and courage to say it, only, according to Orozco, a prophetic sense, will produce great fresco art.

Or perhaps we can phrase it differently. We are builders. We build great walls, and we know that they need painting, pictures, to complete their significance. Fresco, the only kind of painting that becomes a part of the wall itself, the kind of painting best fitted to hold Time at bay, must come to be the accepted method of completing our walls with pictures. But those pictures will match our structures, match the glory of this continent as a Whitman dreamt it, only when at length America dares to give allegiance to heroic ideas, to daring thoughts, to original philosophies. When America, which gave the world some of its most precious gifts in the days when a handful of men, defying earth's greatest Empire, dared dream of a new freedom and bring a new Republic to birth — when America again has gifts of such worth for mankind, the ferment of great art will appear, and great artists will appear to make the glory of high thought visible to all men. For such art only great walls, and "the only manner of painting fit for a man," will suffice.

There is hope. There is, I believe, the certainty of great American frescoes in times to come but not far distant.